SAGACITY OF WOMANHOOD

By

RITCHIE FELIX

COPYRIGHT PROHIBITION:

ISBN 978-1452819815

Published in the United States of America

Ritchie@before40.com

DEDICATION

I dedicate this book to my Mentor Mr. F.E. Isaac, who picked me up amidst chaos and hopelessness in my tender age. He provided me with the shoulders of a scholastic giant on whom I stand today to rule my world. And to my Idol of Womanhood- Chief (Mrs.) Sarah Nwankwo Kalu Ola of the blessed memory who stood by me in the raining season of my life. How I wish you are here to see this epoch-making you started some decade ago in my life. Great Mother, I missed you really much.

ACKNOWLEDGEMENT:

To my Heavenly Father, I give thanks for Grace, inspiration and guidance.

To Ritchie Christie, my Pristine Queen of inestimable value, creating the enabling home environment that inspired the successful completion of this work.

To authors of many great works whose creativity gave me the trajectory to ride on this eternal path of immortality. You are the real phenomena in this ontological void- planet earth.

To Rev. P.K. Emeaba, the First Superintend of Assemblies of God church, Aba North District, Aba Abia State. You are really a spiritual Mentor indeed. You opened me up to sound ethical values with unique standard.

To Surveyor Jay Onwukwe, my chairman at 'Before40.com for Better Citizenship', your

Corporate mentorship is second to none I have seen.

To Obike Ihechiluru, my best friend, Presiding Pastor and whose mentorship about seeming the possibilities in every challenge has been of great value to my rising this far.

To Mrs., Esther Igbeaku, a Mother of great virtues and a Mother worth having a Million time. You taught me to believe at tender age that no condition is permanent.

Thanks to all my great good friends that the space here will not be enough to mention and million thanks to my Publisher.

INTRODUCTION

The institution of womanhood gives lives Neoteric meaning to make Meteoric rise in the affairs of life. Men come in pages of book and women come in sizes of books and in phases of faculties. It is "**parlous**" (wicked) of a kind to relegate to the background, woman! A "**lee Lon**" (One who can make life worth-living for others) that have Pleroma (fullness) of God's "**G"race** ("G"= God in the "race" of life). It is "**phronesis**" (wisdom) to describe a woman not as an individual but as an institution with faculties of "**fecundity**" (fruitfulness) and loaded with "**apocalypse**" (revelation) as department that surpasses the five senses of humanity.

The most potent inheritance or gift of the richest, strongest and most influential man of the century is a woman of **"Charis"** (grace) filled with "**Chara**" (joy) and "**hikanotes**" (God's ability) to make good use of her conscience and super conscious mind to make her marriage fulfilled. Such is a woman sagacity of the fathomless order.

The name: "WOMAN" do not suggest weakling, lack of initiatives or programmed to sit below in life. Rather, this epic masterpiece is set to dissolve ignorance, limitations and labels wrongly placed on womanhood.

This masterful artistic intelligence will help you see beyond your "**dialogismos**' (imagination) and be "**makarios**" (blessed) beyond the human description. You must take charge of your life and have "**egkiateia**" (self-control) to define for your self a noble course that set you apart and empowers you with genuine wealth ad infinitum.

Making fortune is about doing it right by way of discovering your true identity, developing your highly priced potentials in the crucibles of life opportunities, and deploying it to accumulating pretty penny overtime and get yourself flushed with megabucks cum most incredible success. Create your own income grid within your hobby, talents, and distilled potentials and get awash with most expensive currency of freedom in the universe. You can beat the status quo and "**metamorphose**" (a newness of life, a complete change of form, character, appearance or condition) by awakening the deep seated within you. What your monthly check reads is a complete dichotomy to your actual worth in life. You are far bigger than that in both genetic make ups and intellectual prowess. Get transmitted by the deep in you crying for expression.

Sagacity of womanhood is not another intellectual hype on the block, rather **"Uberrima fides**" (sincerity) of inestimable content to enable every woman launch herself into "**recrementitiou**s" (surplus), and superabundance of the best provisions of life.

It is my claim to expertise and exceptional contribution to womanhood the real phenomenon of life. I give it to you with all pleasure. There are far reaching "**guerdons**" (rewards) if you "**lambano**" (receive) these classic and ebullient nuggets loaded in the pages of this Book. **"Chara"** (joy)!

RITCHIE FELIX

PURPOSE

1. The Fine gold of South African is great, but not stronger in superiority to the great faith of those women who survived the apartheid. Though the Buckingham Palace is filled with purest gold but not as great in purity as the loving mind of the great Queen. A woman's love is stronger than death, and her care goes beyond the barricades of norms. Her hands have cradled the birth of excellence to shut up mediocrity in the market place. What a sage, what a gender, and what a sagacity of breed.

2. To be called a woman is a function of birth, and do not suggest weakling. To be a woman indeed is a question of choice and should not be abandoning to fate. Womanhood has suffered great pain for ages for lack of true identity. Who is responsible for this label? Who is the one that place limitation on the mother of earth? Background is not limitation. Woman wake up to rule your world and be that light radiating the paths of greatness, leadership and might. There is nothing like superior gender in the original archive of mother creation, but there is one on whose shoulders lies the rest of great men in life.

There is one whose fecundity is breaking down borders and reaching out to the far ends of the universe giving smile to the faces of hopeless children, casualties of wars, rebellious leadership and corrupt system. DFID- the Queen's greatest universal import. Love- The greatest force simmering the earth orbit yet looked in the void of womanhood.

3. Your Life's most powerful; within-reach secret is the gift of love. Womanhood is the hub of comfort giving direction to a dying world. Live at the altitudinous latitude of love; have altitude of giving love and make the world a better place. Be filled with Chara (joy), **"Pleroma"** (fullness) of Charis (grace), possession of something good that makes the world bask in the euphoria of hopefulness.

4. Womanhood suggest "**hikanotes**" (God's ability), **zoopoie**o (Make drive) of "**auterki**a" (Sufficiency) in view of the fact that your grace is proceeding from beyond the comets that spawn the constellations. Woman, you are from a superior planet where only **Lee Lon** (one who can make life worth living for others) lives. Have worthiness as password for good and enchanting character devoid of all signs of ferociousness or self-assertiveness as little minds do shut the doors against indecency, resist oppression and

join forces with the **phronesis** (wisdom) that rules the future. There your prominence lies.

5. A woman's love is rustic, her mind is filled with more precious pearls than the earth can boost of, and her **phronesis** (wisdom) commands the order that rules the universe. Womanhood has the **dunamis** (might) to effect a sustainable change in far countries of Ethiopia, Somalia, and Rwanda and within the national borders. Men makes love to inflate their ego, but women makes love to stabilize emotions that keeps the earth in the right motion. It is **parlous** (wicked) to hate a woman that is **parlous** (pregnant) with destiny and great ideas to save the world a pain.

6. 70% of world poor people are women between the ages of 15-45yrs- A report released by Amnesty International Published by DIFID, UK Development Hub for the world. These women lives in the worst devastating plight ever, many subjected to varying pedigree of sexual assault by their captors and Lords. This is a callous plight that posts traumatic emotions in the institution of womanhood in the 21st Century. There is no American woman, Europe woman and African woman, but there is only one people, one creature of purpose, one anatomy with same body chemistry of emotion, and one people call woman.

7. The slap on the cheek of African slaves is the greatest undoing of womanhood in this millennium. The assault on Ethiopia woman is a great bruise on women personality across the globe. For if we live now in a global village,

a technological myth, crafted to bring our farthest neighbor closer, why keep quiet in the heat of wickedness unleashed upon a fellow earth citizen- a woman of fate. If we leave them to fate- surely they fade away into the void, but we can give them a name, so that they know someone cares and love. Arise oh women- save the poor and less privileged plummeted in far away Africa. This is not just a call for help, but a wake up call to responsibility. Arise with this **dunamis** (might) to save the world a great pain.

8. A woman is not a tool, not an object of emotions, and not a laboratory to run various sexual experiments. Change that label by your character, shut your doors against degradation and dehumanization of humanity of purpose. From **albinitio** (beginning) women have never been a tool or bag full of tool kits to satisfy men, rather women have always been there to bridge the gap between humanity, nature and the empty void. You are the best product of the Master Architect from whom the universe proceeded. You are not small, you are to be minded and respected, even if you have lost your mind and nobility. You are simply a novelty

waiting to happen. Yes you can! You are a novelty by creation, and a celebrity in the making. Give yours an expression.

9. Womanhood is not defined by shape, structure or body anatomy but by purpose. Womanhood is not a thing to be abandon on the altars of fate, rather a choice to be made in the early hours of your life. Though some are born with testis in between their legs yet they live in a woman's world of reality. Others are born without testis, yet, live in a man's world. Life is all about purpose and rest upon the tripod stand point of ideology from which we choose operate from.

10. Womanhood is not defined correctly by activity, bustle, and quotient of performance or productivity. Such definition is a set up to reduce the true purpose a woman represents in the archives of creation. You can surely rule your world not by terror, but by adding values to life. You have "**hikanotes**" (God's ability) to live a lifestyle of "**auterkia**" (sufficiency) to fill the ontological void planet earth with **Pleroma** (fullness) of "**philo**" (love).

11. Womanhood is not defined by the ability to deliver a baby of same form and kind, but by the ability to be **parlous** (pregnant) and deliver great ideas that rule the world. To

have a human baby is to be trusted with a responsibility of note, but to have an idea nurtured till gestation is far more greater a responsibility that only divine **dunamis** (might) can afford. To have a human baby, have sex, and sex very well, but to have an idea that can change the World, save the world a great pain, add value to lives, and make the world a better place-go beyond sex.

12. To reclaim back the failed states of the world, start with women and children, to breakdown the state art start with the women, and to fight poverty and push the boundaries of corruption far beyond reach start with yourself. You can conquer the world if you first conquer yourself. You can revive the dead if you first revive the deeds on the inside of you. You can change lives out there on the streets from Asia to African Caribbean's to Australian, and from America to Europe- only if you can change yourself first. The most deadly terrorist resides with you; but you can conquer with focus, vision and a mission statement that you bet your life on. Who say you are a woman? Who dare call you a weakling? Remove that wrong label.

BEAUTY & SEX

13. Every single act of sex drill away calories of energy that can be transmitted into a choice equivalent of financial break through. To have sex early in the day is good but in the early hours of your womanhood. Early morning sexual rendezvous is great only if it is not in the early morning of your life. For it is evil to birth what you cannot nurture, and sheer callousness to fill the world with problems.

14. Sex is the cheapest commodity in the world market places and market spaces today, yet comes at a price. There is sexual act that comes with a personal price, and there is that, that have generational negative impact. If you must zip down your skirt, zap for a good condom, and if you must zip up, get to the zenith of good conduct. For going down to between or below only takes less than an hour and a condom, but going up and staying above in life require a lifetime mission statement with definite serum of conduct.

15. Sex relaxes the nerves, enchants the mind, soothes pains and give you that boost to ride on the turf of pressures of life only if it done within the paradigm of marriage. It is good to match a tender loom or to "tender loom", skin to skin, blood to blood only when most caution

is observed. You cannot eat your cake, and have it back. Kiss the butt only if it is clinically certified.

16. The greatest sex position that give the highest pleasure ever is the position of the mind during intercourse. Men make love to faces while women make love to the mind. Men are obsesses by sex but women are enchanted by love. To have sex is cheap and easier than to show love. Superiority of gender is more a function of progress than that sheer act of benevolence attached to sex.

17. Beauty is vain; if it comes without a character, definite, mission of course, one that can add value and personal willingness to serve humanity. Beauty is malicious if is used as a

tool to spread virus and unleash fear upon humanity. Beauty is useless if it is not useful to itself first. Beauty is both in the eyes of the beholder and that of the carrier.

18. Beauty and sex are both twins that can start a relationship in the morning, ask for divorce in the noon and eat the scourge of sorrows and regrets in the evening. Both beauty and sex can be suppressed to give destiny vent to express itself. Beauty can fade with time in the market place but not in the eyes of beholder, likewise sex can be denied, yet not

in the minds of individual. A woman of noble purpose tames herself to enhance her profitability.

19. Others can have sex, but not you, other can smoke “crack” but not you, others can get involve but not you, why? You are a cherished species of woman hood, wonderfully made, and loaded with gifts, grace and intelligence. You are unique so do not follow others

20. The night after wedding ceremony is night full with bliss and has the **Pleroma** (fullness) of divine support and **hikanotes** (God’s ability). It is a night true women grant their spouse to encrypted code to decipher their difference in the world of womanhood, to see through an exclusive rights in a see-through gown, packed full with distinctive excellence and a life time investment of purpose guided with absolute jealousy though amidst animalistic impulses that crops madness out of many women.

21. The wedding ring is vain if it lacks the fire of emotion and the touch of excellence. You can hardily amend broken integrity, but you can start all over again. High school love

is as good as high school risk to gamble your future out of balance. Teenage sex eccentrics tilt the life original purpose for young people, and perhaps shop the capacity to incapacitate good potentials while drilling hope away from them. The wedding bell is good as along as it rings for pleasure and warns the prospective contractors or both parties about to wed.

22. Do not marry out of pity so that you do not later find yourself in the pit of regrets. Do not marry out of sheer recommendation except after evaluating values and other interesting factors that meet your need in a wife or husband. It is far better and less expensive to work on your marriage to work, than to work on divorce. Divorce may appear a good option out of a temporary crisis in marriage but never a best option in a mean time.

23. Pressure of marriage challenges is a true test of commitment on both parties involved in the union. Do not forget passion is cheap, but compassion comes out at a price. A woman is saddled with far greater a responsibility to make her marriage work better and for the better of the two involved, than the man. Pressure that comes with pregnancy pulls much more gravity than that involved in providing for the family. It is the man that is expected in most cases to provide money, shelter and food for the

home, but the woman provides the right atmosphere to nurture the family and cultivates the bliss of the matrimony. Marriage is beyond the primordial eroticism of sex and greater in force than the tiara of mental enchantment. Yet, marriage cannot do without sex.

24. All a woman need is **phronesis** (wisdom) and **epignosis** (involve oneself with responsiveness) to chart a distinct course in the complex world of womanhood. Be full of skill and **"Charis"** (grace) in dealing with others. Release your **dunamis** (ability) to serve others- for in doing this you add up values for yourself. A woman that lend support to others pile up support for self. A woman full of "**Chrestotes**" (right distinction in personality, placidness, righteousness and goodness) is always full of potency to champion the course of a sustainable change. Uncommon character espoused to **epignosis** (involve yourself with responsiveness) is an inestimable level that is not common place in the market place of the world. It is **phronesis** (wisdom) to be good even when it is not convenient.

25. Beauty is best when it is located in the brain of a woman than on her anatomy or body configuration. It is vain thing to have beauty devoid of good brain, nay, and productive brain. The breakdown of several institutions of marriage usually results more from the lack of good brain than for

lack of beauty. Woman thou are lose!-Bishop T. D. Jakes declared. To stay glued to status quo is a choice, and to expand your tool kits to increase your options in life is by far a better "**guerdon**" (reward) for giving into "**apocalypse"** (revelation) of the eternal values that rules over the universe.

26. Sex is sacred, and must be treated with dignity. It is a slap on womanhood to strip naked in a TV commercial just for money. It is a suggestion for lack of true concept of money. Money is both as much entity and as a universal concept. The corporate world turns idea into money, and not a woman into money. Nudity is not synonymous as idea or money. Bearing it all before the staring eyes before platinum screen only suggest a lack of understanding, nay, and lack of respect for womanhood. Obviously, sex is better in a movie because life is a movie itself albeit, running without a script in the hands of any men. Movies are packaged for adults who sports interest to have it at any give away cost, but a TV commercial is cheap and abysmally degrading in status.

27. Have sex with good conviction especially when you are prepared to handle any possible outcome. To say No to sex with animal is **phronesis** (wisdom) and reflects sagacity of true womanhood of the order of "**apocalypse"** (revelation)

that is beyond the constellations of human faculties. To go through life depending on tools of sex to eke out living is as good as taking a voyage through the destructive abyss of immortality. You have something more productive than "sex-hawking" in you that is called "BRAIN". God tugged it deep inside your skull to enable you beats the oddities of life and enthrone your destiny.

28. More women of great virtues have died for failure to resourceful engaged their brains at work than for lack of talents and skill. There is always a limit to which commercial sex-hawking can take a woman but still at a gruesome price. Having sex with a man do not suggest to him that you love him, rather proves to him that you can moan for the pleasure of his strokes, and that you can satisfy his sexual cravings cum misadventures. Whenever you sex outside marriage, it takes value and good life away from you. Do not be deceived by anything!

29. Sex can boost your ego within marriage, but you have to pay the price that will keep the experience with you always. It is a commitment that you learn with time. Sex can abort a great destiny and cage potentials down six feet's if you do it with a stranger, especially, if he has HIV-Aids. It is far greater a terrorism to flaunt bare your hidden womanhood

to the public in fabrics of fashion devoid of dignity for womanhood.

30. If a woman is hot, it is good if the hotness harness the potentials lucked up in her brain than reduce her true value at the market place.

31. Hot quickie produces hot outcomes, and heated romantic pleasure produces hated regretful treasure a times. Womanhood is the hub of humanity that orbits the future constellations of any generation and for all sapience sense. Have the sixth sense but not the sixth insatiable sense of sensuality. Have a strong affinity to show love to others, but not lovemaking in TV commercials.

32. Whatever a woman is willing to show to the public is exactly what she is willing to share with the public. Whatever you put on your thinking cap is actually a determinant on how you will be addressed in life. Most influential women and richest women on earth do not invoke themselves mischievous lifestyle before cameras to avoid lost of value and relevance in the marketplace.

33. Richest women do have sex but often a time in a more descent and dignifies way to keep the lead. Not all rich

women possess their body in order. A nymphomaniac is not good for role model and not good for womanhood. The strongest of all women rule their world by instrumentality of the brain than by mortal tool of Mother Nature. Choose one with which to take your world by surprise. For the earnest expectation of Sons of Men is waiting for the manifestation of the Sons and Daughters of most High God of Heaven. Unlock that goldmine seeking for expression within you.

WEALTH & POWER

34. The most potent time to mine the gold nuggets loaded on your inside is now, not tomorrow. Have "**phronesis**" (wisdom) of the available resources at your disposal, discover, develop and deploy at work to amass wealth for yourself. Think globally and act locally to stay relevance and marketable in the global parlance of values. The whole world is your laboratory, is your theatre and is your marketplace. Take charge of your life and the dream you are created for.

35. You must discover the wealth secret principle that works for you and flush you with resounding success before your 30 years, and get hold on this threshold of stupendous riches in your forties, live the dream of your life and immortalized your name sixties and seventies. Then when you are 100, leave an indelible imprint on the sands of time by teaching others what you thick and immortal. Your children will be many and will not forget you for generations to come.

36. Control the resources in your possession, invest it wisely and match your wealth tree grow into thick branches to carry any financial weight. Great people of the earth are known for their ability to groom scarce resources into abundant resources. If you can increase the value of anything, the whole world will surely beat a path to your gate. By nature, a woman is endowed to multiple whatever things given to her.

37. Sincerity and Integrity are both great assets to turn your insignificant gift, skill and idea into great asset. The richest and most influential women of the century trades here intangible values to get flushed with riches and wealth of varying pedigree.

38. All women are equal is an age long sage of humanity in the parlance of human rights and justice. All women are equal by birth, but some are greater in status than other by reason of the course they choose to run in life. Great women of the century choose greatness by choice and not by a mere chance. Pay the price to translate

your hidden values into its physical cash equivalence. A woman of great economic value is a great economic value is a great asset to her generation in her society and beyond.

39. The instinct for sexual rendezvous in adult woman resides in the same faculty as the intellect she needs to create her riches and make her name famous in the society. The ability to lock up this instinct to enable it reach a credos before transmitting its into its physical cash equivalence is what separates the women from the females. Great decision lead to great life and shallow mindset leads to shallow life and shabby ends meet.

40. You do not need people endorsement to become great. You need to endorse yourself worth, accept yourself and celebrate yourself before others do so to you. Nobody reduce or assault you without your consent directly or indirectly. Get hold of your life, take charge, and control what happens and when to happen. This way you use the harshest turf of tides of life to ride yourself to stardom and great riches.

41. You do not need a Buckingham Palace to become a Queen of your life, but you surely need caution and life precepts of the Buckingham Palace to become a celebrated Queen of your dream. Take time before the mirror to dress gorgeously as a time princess, walk like a Queen, and bridle your tongue like a Queen then, you are 40% into your journey of your dream. Guide your integrity jealously and take time to fix your own palace where only you shall be celebrated.

42. You do not need to be rich as the Queen to keep your good carriage in public glare, rather you need to be rich in **"phronesis"** (wisdom) as the Queen you need not to spend so much on brand and fashion fads to be accepted, rather you do need to dress the way you want to be address. You can create your own fashion, brand and rules of the game. You do not need swim the tides of fashion current, go ahead and come out with your own label.

43. Over dependence on the provision of a boyfriend or ex-spouse kills ingenuity within a woman. What if the ex-spouse is insane or

reprimanded in prison, or even dead- you surely live your life and explore the latent potentials resident within you. Do not forget job means Just-over-broke what you need to sustain life and relevance is called work. A successful woman looks for a work after she has secured a job.

44. Job is searched for but work is usually created by the one who want it. Job pays you peanuts monthly or per hour, but work may not pay you immediately. Go ahead and nurture it till you cradle it to maturity where it begins to pay you in monetary equivalence and money stereotypes. You surely become financially free, and retire young by working for yourself.

45. The Power and influence of a woman is her true worth in the market place and in the achievement parlance of her generation. If you are laid off your job, do not lay yourself off from work. What you need to live your dream is not salary but a fortified income system or networks of residual incomes.

46. If your mind is often flushed with ideas, you can be flushed with cash and success. Your mind is your biggest tool ever to enthrone you in life, perhaps if you are smart, your enthronement comes ahead of your contemporary. To have your mind loaded with divine hunches is a suggestion that you are chosen to lead the pack.

47. The School system issues certificate honors to graduates on exit from the institution, but glossary white paper lacks the potency to define who or what you actually become in real life. You can win the race of life from behind if you have the "Grace "G" stand for God in the race of life. For since competitors can challenge and compete with your intelligent as well as with your charismatic prowess, but never can they compete with level of "G-"race upon your life.

48. Know who you need in your life before you 25yrs, tap into his/her **"phronesis"** (wisdom) to attain your utmost "**hikanotes**" (God's ability), and "**Zoopoieo"** (Make alive) your wealth and live a lifestyle of "**auterkia"** (sufficiency) in your 30s, and in all the days of your life. The same power to make wealth also sustains health

to "**Pleroma**" (fullness) of the time Mother Nature have endowed you with or imputed into your account at birth. At forties come up with your own "**autogenesis**" (act of knowledge), and become anything you logged into your mind to become. Write your rules, maximize the moment, come out with your script and list yourself on the hall of fame of your generation.

49. Many unsung heroes died full and return to the womb of mother earth unnoticed because they were stopped by the rules. Who made the rule? Who evaluated the makers of the rules?

Life is a stage said William Shakespeare; some follow the rules strictly to their peril, but others great in beauty of their dreams either bends the rules in their favor or create new rules for themselves and end up immortalizing their names in the historic gallery of humanity in this ontological void-planet-earth.

50. The School system is not the only way to riches neither the high streets dilly-dally a gateway to prominence. Take time to build up for yourself aptitudes to reach the altitude of your dream,

travel the attitudes of your mind gaze to actually transverse the cutting edges of competence of your field of specialty, that way, you hone your natural capableness, and be flush with money.

51. Many women run their lives on adrenalin and not "**phronesis**" (wisdom) and understanding. They mistake activity to productivity.

52. The thrills of developing concepts upon concepts, money ideas upon money ideas, and grant contacts that can harness motions of pound sterling, becomes an end to such people instead of the means. Little wonder, hardily do they show forth any sign of productivity. To such people education is usually an end and not seen as the means to cultivate life to get out whatever you want.

RULES GUIDING MONEY MAKING:

53. Money creates money, and gravitates to the one who build strong magnetism around it.

54. Money can give you speed in life. It can work hard for you if you engage it to do so, so never work hard breaking down your system to make money. But you can work smart.

55. Money is both a raw material for execution of project and end product of an investment. It gives the right to ownership of assets if you so wish.

56. Money does not answer to a problem, rather answers to a feasible project. Right use of money and money-making skill upgrades value of the owner, but wrong use of money or its skill reradiates it owner.

57. Money makes as much friends as much enemies. It is a tool to recreate a woman's

world, and give her career acceleration. But it is a weapon in the hand of a gal who is skirt-driven. The one color of money is the one the owner gives to it. Start with the one in your possession now.

58. Money is a reward for labor but not true parameters to ascertain the actual worth of value of the laborers.

59. Money is a reward for problem solved. If you want more money, solve more problems around, and you shall be rewarded for your service.

60. Do not bargain or negotiate a business when you are hungry so that you do not sell your most cherished financial future for a dime by signing it away with your signature.

61. Many great boxers of great achievement while in the ring are today financial Eskimos looking for a way of survival because they were actually much interested in the fighting than the productivity that comes with. This way, many sign away great fortune in the future to the mere promoters.

Some boxers, though alive suffers major health crisis but there promoters keep securing major financial deals in the market places.

62. Money can be use in two ways:

(a) Buy the future by investing it to secure assets and creates major consistent cash flows

(b) Sell your future by spending it on liabilities like buying cars, womanizing, chasing after boyfriends, wearing fashion brands, funfair and costly jamborees. Money can get you into or out of trouble. It can elongate life or shortens it cycle.

63. You must have "**egkrateia**" (self control) to maximize the economic value of your money, money-making skills and acquired assets to stay on top of your game. You have to flutter, "**Hagar**" (meditate) on the truth money is the artificial transmutation of your hunch into its physical financial equivalence.

64. Money is the brain child of mankind so follow the principles that attract it and be "**Makarios"** (blessed) "**ad infinitum"** (endless)

WOMAN IN THE JOB -LABOUR MARKET OF 21ST CENTURY

65. The rules that govern the Job market have changed with time, events and other circumstances beyond the control of humanity. The 21st century economic climate demands all hand on desk, and leaving no room for gender-consideration in most cases. Learn the rules and follow it strictly or write your own "**autogenesis**" (self knowledge) to either influence the existing rules or completely abhor them.

66. Every single vacancy anywhere has over two thousand persons gumming for it in your locality across the earth vast expensive space.

67. The continuous innovation of information and communication technologies has to a large extent over-stretched the limits of virtually every organization or industrial working or operational realities. At such, the internet now determines most strategies use in both the

Marketplaces and market spaces respectively. This alone has cost many unprepared folks their jobs. Employers now de-emphasize gender issues to hammer much more emphasis on suitability for the job in quote.

CREDIBILITY:

Credibility is an imperative for any woman who expects to produce result with ease in the knowledge Age. It is an essential part of every woman life, especially for those who aspire to the top of their career or field. Credibility is the magical wand that can make any woman produce result with sublime ease where others are failing. It is a necessary tool for uncommon achievement in the 21st Century.

68 Credibility is tool to gain the trust of others and authority to perform beyond the widest imagination of your world. With credibility you can rule your world and keep the ball always rolling in your favour no matter the odds.

69 You may not need to break any Bank, but always wear expensive shoes and not fads that can easily go out of vogue. Dress with wisdom and make yourself most comfortable while in any attire.

70 A woman that is in charge always wears confident to the marketplace and accepts responsibility for all actions. This surely makes her credible before her critics.

71 It is right to make your sheer confidence outweigh your many doubts to give you the confidence of others, especially, when there is need for a competent leadership where you work. People tend to move with the soul that has all the statistics and the arts to move beyond any perceptible limitation.

72 In speeches and in conversations never use vulgar language on others; it is capable of stripping of your profitability and credibility respectively. A king or Queen is never expected to use foul words on others.

73 Strive to make yourself impeccable in words and in actions. Be prepared to flaunt your clear intentions before the press at any given time. Never any one opportunity to insult you or your intelligence. Find an intelligent route out any perceived fracas that dirt your dignity.

74 Make it a life rule to show respect to people no matter the odds involved, and do this with utmost sincerity of the mind. Never go after your critics no matter how right you might be in your own judgment. Use silent as your ultimate weapon to defeat your enemies all the time.

75 Never append your signature on any document you do understand its content. It is even wise to sleep over issues overnight before your endorsement. It is

a way to protect your credibility in the marketplace of life.

76 It is important for a woman of great means and value abhor sleeping around with men and avoid been caught pant-down before the camera no matter what or who is involved. One mistake can take more than a Century to cover or manage.

77 Fight your flesh to tell the truth always because truth is the catalyst that hype your credibility in a competitive environment and keep you ahead of others with bloated persona. One lie can degrade your net worth in the marketplace and can be very difficult to regain.

78 A woman of great credibility is quiet an asset of inestimable value in her organization. She can be the reason the customer list swell astronomically. She is the right face to make presentation of the company new product or service. The people buy you first before the product no matter it features and benefits.

79 Credibility of a woman is always reflective in her choice posture all the time. It is wise and advisable

for a woman with "**Pleroma'** (Fullness of Grace) to sit confidently and be cheerful in the public to make her the center of attractiveness amidst the millions of others present. That is credibility!

80 The best way to access a man of your crave is to flaunt your credibility when the opportunity calls and not to attempt enchanting him with your bare nudity. It is wrong and always remains wrong no matter the reason adduce for this error. Sure enough, you end up reducing the chances of being considered credible next time.

81 Do you know people are mindful to notice the care that you give to your skin, teeth and your legs the first time they meet you? You do not have the second chance to prove to them otherwise next time that you see them.

82 A woman with heavy chest Pointers and well rounded-balanced waistline, but is character-deficient is a minus to her world and to her organization. It is important for a woman of means learn to control her tongue same way she consciously control her undulating buttocks.

83 To keep your credibility, each time you shop keep upgrading the quality of your wardrobe not necessarily with expensive fashions but with good clothes.

MONEY

Money remains the biggest reason that people have expanded options for survival in the corporate world. It is reason behind the hot chase for upgrade in the university certificate in the corporate world. The instant chase for businesses in Asia and India by Europe and the United States at the moment is predicated on money or more money. The firm or individual that continue to combine effectiveness in skillfulness and leveraged knowledge based on the evolving technological hype of the Marketplace at the present will inevitably lead to generation of unending supply of money.

84 The ancient secret for wealth creation is to understudy others who have made it in the area that you want to make your adventure or field of specialty. You have to read at least 5 to 10 financial journals or magazine monthly.

85 Being very diligent at work will make you money, but not as much you need to lush in wealth. Rather you need to become very diligent in updating your skills and antics of money making to be in real unlimited supply of money.

86 In the corporate setting you need to be in the service or sales division to make the income of your dream. You need to use the company's platform to build good relationship that can sustain you even when you are no longer there. The real profit any sale is the repeat sale.

87 To achieve financial freedom within a short time, make your money work real harder than you always, and take the joy of making advance payment to your supplier to earn great discount and endeared you to their mind. This way you build profitability even without much ado.

88 As a CEO of your company, pay your employee very well and before the end of the month, this work like a sort of magic to improve on their commitment and diligence respectively. Inability to pay your employees very well will cause apathy and paralysis of ingenuity of workers.

"Beyond Sex: "What Most Influential and Richest People Sees In Marriage"

Sex is not enough to deliver all the expectations and bliss of a marital union. Sex lubricates the nerves but do not decode the inscription of the mind. The faculties that destroy marriages do not succumb to tender sex-maniacs neither regard macabre dance of eroticism. What holds any relationship is not sex, but understanding of parties involved, enrolling in the school of fecundity to explore the gallery of sexuality is vein thing to do when the conscience of contractors of sex is sealed with selfishness.

The most influential and richest people see something bigger than sex in marriage. They see values or value system that can be both productive and sustaining in the discourse of life. They go for it and this account for about 60% of their greatness. Sex illuminates the mind, relaxes the thinnest vessels in the upper hemisphere of man brain. Sex is a balm of healing, soothes pain and provides emotional balance for traumatize people. Sex is a bodily exercise, nay, yoga to actual gaining tripartite consciousness into the metaphysical blues of the cosmic rendezvous. Riding the wings of emotion sparked by plateau of adrenalin dripping with diorama of chromatin is a wonderland of unlimited possibilities and infinite blues call it nth faculty of sensuality.

You can conquer your world if you conquer yourself. You can rule your world if you first rule yourself. You can live your dreams if you zip up your trousers. If you must zip down get good condom, and if you must go up in life get good conduct. Woman fecundity is both bucolic and romantic, but much more destructible in the bosom of a wrong gal. More men, great in virtues and wonderful in their dreams-have died in the bosom of women, than in the bloodiest strike of terrorism. Sex develops and envelopes a dream, a woman bosom bears children as much as, it spits venomous poison to kill her victims.

The grave is six-Feet because it swallows up only the body, but a woman bosom is far greater in dept because it swallows a man, his dreams unborn. Sex is not everything but heals everything. Making love early in the morning is good, but not in the early morning of your life. Sex is good for Las Vegas posh Daddies and even more rustic for the Beverly Hill pop stars. Sex or lovemaking in the early hours of your life can mar and demeans your very existence. For if the purpose of a thing is not known abuse becomes unavoidable. Porn sex is good if it can also show you the anatomy of your future.

The most influential and the richest uses sex either as a weapon for or against pleasure. Beyond sex are the faculties of true relationship. Sex is not a sign that "he" loves you, rather a suggestion that you can satisfy his sexual cravings. Sex is not marriage, but there can never be a marriage without sex. Sex is not limited by bodily contact, sex is digital as it is dignifying. Mental intercourse procreates more than other forms of sex. Sex is the University of Creation that has not graduated its first students.

Everybody enroll into the institution stays as undergraduate till his or her demise. Sex is neither a true measurement for manhood nor an impeccable parameter to ascertain true love. But sex can be a ready yardstick to attest the strength of any woman. The strength of a man is located around his upper body chambers while the power of a woman is at the lower cavity of their body; the strength of a woman is located on the lower part of her body. The greatest warrior among men in life is a senior slave of a woman at the closet. Great Warriors wobbles at his feet on the sight of a revealed woman laps. To me, this is the immutable weaponry in the arsenal of Mother Nature. Kingdoms go into captivity when the kings drop their crowns to worship the bosom of a woman.

Sex appears to be the cheapest commodity in the market place of the world today, but know it is a viral load of arsenal that will finally ditch our world into the oblivion.

If you have headache, get sex for your healing, but also get true love in the process for nothing saves like love. If you are confuse, get sex to relax and re-focuses yourself but also make a commitment to love or get shattered next time. The fiercest terrorist love and shows love to a woman, but not lust any woman. A woman can be anything and anything can be a woman too. What you show yourself makes her the Queen of your life. Whatever thing that shares the magnitude of love for a woman in your life become also a woman to you, that is why, some romances with "war-arms". Check out what you have, so that you either go under or beyond the valley of sex. If you must sex a woman do not forget the rule: "You must sex her very well" or throw your life into Hell. It is a choice that the world richest and most influential has made to be where they are now.

STRATEGY, SYNERGY & LOVE.

•Queens lives in palaces and kingdoms across the universe.

The beauty of any kingdom is the presence of a woman whose beauty surpasses that of Angel because of her most inner beauty that cannot be deciphered by an electromagnetic manipulation.

•Buckingham palace is touching the ends of earth by just

the finger of love of the great Queen. It is error of a kind to have several women in the under-developed Nations of the world under slavery and cultural bondage when their pristine position is the palaces in high places of the earth.

Womanhood is a crown to humanity and unfathomable blessing wrapped in fragile vessel.

- The life of any man is hollow and empty without a woman, nay, a virtuous queen. The Buckingham Palace is great in beauty not of its precious myriad of gold, silver and pearls, but for the beauty of the Great Queen – whose beauty and love knows no bound and spawns the orbit of the entire universe. Beauty is not a thing of the eyes, rather a colour code of the mind; in a spiritual sense, it is not static, it is digital and travels faster than the speed of light.

- Beauty is a strong strategy of kind; it is the strongest weapon of a woman and the indomitable arsenal of development in the world of Queens living in their

Buckingham Palaces across the earth. The Buckingham Palace of England is touching the ends of the earth with LOVE, and snatching human-preys from the claws of their predators. The twin radicals of development: Ukaid and British Council are doing the entire world better than what the eyes filters from pages of newspapers. It is the golden import of a Queen whose love knows no bound.

•Love is the best way to spell a woman's beauty. The

colour code of womanhood is beauty expressed in humanitarian love spread across the earth axes. It is good for a woman to possess her world by her worth in the market place of love, nay, and humanitarian love shown to fellow earth citizen. This kind of love builds up and never cracks any down.

• Womanhood is the ageless epitome of love, and remains the pristine crown of humanity on planet earth wrapped in succulent vessel, loaded with psychological hype, clothed with voluptuous flesh, red with love, pale with mind emotions, pregnant with burdens of cares, and speaks with distinctive excellence that fills the ambience with ebullience of sapience – is the creature called WOMAN!.

• Bodily beauty is not enough to make a queen out of you on the absence of inner beauty. Bodily beauty can give any woman a bed in the home of any man or lover, but you can become a Queen anywhere in the world if you have proven inner beauty. What sustains a Buckingham Palace is not beauty of the flesh but that of the mind. Kingdoms that outlived the builders are founded on inner beauty of uncommon Queens. Bodily beauty alone kills and kills faster than HIV/Aids, but inner beauty sustains and springs with abundant life. It is far better and more profitable to build ones life as a woman or "**world-man**" on bricks of good character and sustained inner beauty, than to loaf away in idleness of thoughts or fads.

- You can turn your corner of the earth into something far better and magnificent than Buckingham Palace of England if only you consciously wire yourself with right inner beauty. Spiritually speaking, Buckingham Palace is a derivative of an inner beauty expressed in golden character, distinctive excellence of sustained vision with treasure of mission statements without measure. You may not have the privilege to step into the golden gates of Buckingham Palace in England, but you can build or clone one around your own corner of the globe if you so wish to by possessing the right colour code of the Queen's mind.

- It is vain to sit over a Kingdom or over any people

without inspiring them to personal fulfillment of life purpose. It is inglorious to be eaten up by ones self position or possession that you can hardily raise a second you. Everything begins and ends with leadership submitted by John Maxwell (All time Leadership Maestro). It is better you make more friends of values than you make more.

- You owes yourself success, love & care to be the Queen

of your life. There is no limitation anywhere in the world except in the thesis and antithesis of men. A woman that knows her real endowment takes her world by storm to reach her envious destination in life. Limitation is better spelt as determination in a woman's world.

•Great men rises and goes down the history lane, yet the arbiter of his greatness remain feeble and weak in her national state. The Shakespearean Macbeth was a valiant Soldier because of the fearless woman he has at home. He conquers his enemies in the battlefield after first submitting to the drills of his clever wife at home. The home in the hands of a clever woman can become anything great. She can turn the home into a theatre to brood her intellectual wares; she can turn it into military academy. She can turn it into a place of rearing genius.

- Womanhood is not a thing to be despised, but a thing to be coveted by all and sundry. It is a marathon to be completed only if you are to sport a purpose married to hardwork, nay, and smart work. The entire universe tends to be dominated by men, but woman dominates the men, and influence virtually every cause of his action. A woman is useful in season and out of season, and a catalyst that can speed up any process regardless of its ambient composition and destination.

- No Barrack Obama without a Mitchelle Obama. No Bill Clinton without a Hillary Clinton. No Bill Gates without a Melinda Gates. No Austin Okocha without a Nkechi Okocha. No Goodluck Jonathan without a Patience

Jonathan. No Ritchie without a Christie and… continue the list to build up.

- There is no grate politician atop any ivory toner without a solid support of a wife, mother and lover. The world of a woman is a world clustered with multifaceted responsibilities and multi-dimensional challenges. Yet, the species of humans conquers all and exceed expectations of all to rule the world by ruling the hearts of men who seats over Kingdoms, Conglomerates, Movements and Schools of thoughts.

FIFTY REASONS WHY SOME WOMEN FAIL IN LIFE.

- Lack of definite purpose
- Weak Desire for success
- Incompetence
- Lack of Financial Education
- Insufficient Formal Education
- Lack of Self-Discipline
- Lack of Perseverance
- Lack of Insight and Foresight
- Lack of Sponsorship or funding
- Lack of Mentorship
- Lack of attention and love
- Lack of early training
- Lack of home training

- Lack of Proper self-esteem
- Teenage pregnancy
- Sexual Abuse
- Wrong Selection of a mate in marriage
- Wrong selection of career
- Wrong Association
- Lack of enough enthusiasm to start
- Romance Distraction
- Broken home or broken marriage
- Several marriages
- Inability to stick to one partner
- Fear of poverty
- Fear of criticism
- Fear of lost of love
- Fear of old age
- Fear of death
- Sickness or diseases

- Deformity
- Character Deficiency
- Prayerlessness
- Drunkenness
- Emotional Maladjustment
- Extravagance
- Intolerance
- Lack of Medicare
- Lack of Proper welfare
- Instability of National Polity
- War and terrorism
- Drug Addiction
- Gangsterism/Cultism
- Corrupt leadership of society
- Poor Budgetary for Women Development
- Dragon Policies against women
- Poor culture of Womanhood celebration

- Lack of acceptance
- Marginalization of women in politics
- Wrong dressing culture.

- The ability to face life squarely without buying into any of the excuses above, unleash Excellency out of you naturally. Women who are on top of their arts and games across the earth axes, either managed, setbacks or overcome it out rightly by engaging the inner forces within.

- If you lack Medicare of the State, you get yourself one, if you lack proper welfare, you can declare warfare against every limitation keeping you down to gain place in life. If you are deformed physically, you can stay informed mentally and be informed spiritually.

- If the Government fail to plan and budget for you, you can rise up to plan and make proper budget for yourself. You can decide to quit hard drugs and alcoholism to create a name for yourself on earth. And if you suffer marginalization, then you recreate a befitting image for yourself.

- If you are not celebrated, you own yourself smart movement to a place where you are tolerated and celebrated. You can empty your wardrobe load of poor dresses and re-dress as one on special assignment to rule your world in excellence and superlative accomplishment.

- If you are chains, the skills, knowledge and latent potentials amassed in you cannot be chained- only you can decide to chain it. Apostle Paul of the Holy Scripture in the New Testament wrote several books of the bible in chains.

- If you lacked early training, it is important, you don't lack late training. How you begin life is not important, where you started out on the journey of life is not important, what is important is where you hope to end or targeting to end.

- Incompetence in the field of football should not stop you from trying your hands elsewhere to build up real wealth for yourself. Incompetence is only a reflection that you need to re-train, and acquire the knowledge gap missing to become competent.

Incompetence early in marriage do not suggest quit or divorce, rather suggests that you need to address some fundamental issues to engineer progress to happen.

- What a woman fears often a time never happen, rather what happen is what she fail to do about her fears. Nobody will prosecute you for checking out the price tag of a befitting car, but life will prosecute you for the failure of not checking out the price.

- What any woman needs to go up in life and surprise her peers is in the ability to go the extra mile when others just stop at the average. Go extra mile in whatever you set out to do or in your choice career. For sure – success, greatness, fame and fortune waits out there at the top. All you need to leave the crowd at the bottom is sheer determination and gut to dare the devils out there. You can only if you affirm it with actions.

- Go the extra mile to please a man; he will make you the Queen of his Kingdom and the astute crown of his pride. Once you determine to go the extra mile your latent energy comes alive to achieve your target.

- Womanhood is all about creative vision to extract the creative intelligence and deploy it at work to make you lush in abundance, time and fortune. Creative vision is born of out veracity of desires to be the Queen and not the kill in the kingdom. Creative vision requires diligence, magnetic personality and honesty to leverage on opportunities around.

- You need paper at the onset of your creative vision, but what will help you achieve and sustain your desired outcome is people. Thus, the people are your main business and not the paper.

- To have faith is good for a woman, but not good enough for "Lee Lon" (one who makes things happen good for others) what an agent of change need is called Applied Faith. What makes a "Lee Lon" out of any woman is Applied Faith.

LEADERSHIP EDGE

- You set yourself up for eviction in the school of success if you dare fear competition from others or fear criticism. You can never rise up to your best if you do not face confrontations and criticism that life parades. To be successful any day and at anywhere, you have to prepare to lead others.

- You do not need to mind opposition no matter the fatality or faculty or threat involved, you can always win if you dare major on your position and manage your possession. You can lose your position. Except you begin to mind opposition.

- A woman who is able to organize herself, her house, her works and recline into self-hibernation in the presence of God cannot lose sweetness of her onion any day. The greater the time she spends in the presence of God, the better her sweetness and the greater her success in all her endeavour.

- You cannot fail in life with well-organized details about your set out goals. It is the most beauty of a woman to lead by strong point and not by common sense. You can lead if you have the right and best details about the project or filed of your specialty. You get your pay check for what you do and not for what you know. It is important you go beyond having details.

- What have they got you doing with mere details when you can create actions to decorate your world with most precious pearls of gracefulness? It is doing the right thing at the right time and right season that singles you out as the best and most sagacious sage of your world. It is living in this world of light and rare reality that unveils the sagacity of womanhood – gift of gold from God of all humanity.

- What have they got your ears listening to when there is urgent need to hear the voices of children crying from afar countries of the world whose destinies are enmeshed in waters of hopelessness, emptiness and helplessness? Every leader is a human with two ears but never listen to two conversations at same time. You have the right to choose what to give your ears to, and whatever you listen to at a time either reduces you or lights up your inner beauty to smolder with an uncommon passion to reach out for the dying souls. Woman, Thou art loose, rise up and light up your world. The time to shine and rule your world is now.

- What have they got you reading in your leisure my Queen? Africa is committing genocide and the bone of innocents' liters the streets as befitting bouquets is set before the vultures in the open heavens. The water of crimes, corruption and terrorism sweeps across the entire parlance of the universe and the mothers of the Milky Way cuddles away in romantic extraordinary. What a perplexity? What a shame in a charm of beauty enchanting with illusion of a shame in shanty?

- Where they have got you going in a world of wars and chaos? Every red carpet liters with red pool of blood agog with crimes of leadership: mismanagement of justice, religious imbroglio, rape of intelligence of intellectuals, manslaughter, secret killings, the cash heist, knowledge of heist and technological heist, greed of leaders and human sacrifice in disguise of war. Arise great mothers of the universe, the true test of leadership prowess is not in walking on red carpets but looking sternly at the red faces of human predators dressed in leadership apparel and rebuke the daylight out of those monsters.

- What have they got on your thinking cap amidst the orchestra of man to man wickedness? They have taken the jobs away, looted the economy dry, and taken into slavery our young sons and virgin daughters. Woman, what have they got you thinking – when you undress and paste the screens with nudity? Queens are supposed to be distinctive excellence in character, attitude and platitude of novelty with ebullience of sapience. The art of true money making by a woman of integrity combines mastery of her latent potentials and wealth of inventiveness to reveal her over abounding sagacity that is outstanding in world of intelligence. Absolutely, not the other way round!

- What have they got you addressing when evil is dressed like a choir master in the vestry of human turmoil? Every speech address delivered before any person is either a bond of emancipation or a bond of captivity. Woman, what have they got you addressing? Nobody get you addressing anything without your address and dressing sense. The media wants your attention 24hrs/7days a week to address your beauty, body size, cleavage, pedicure and manicure, sex and sizzling romance when the society lacks Medicare, love, passion for the less privilege, and the motherless. Woman, what have they got you talking about in the recent time?

- What have they got you feeling every day? Your true satisfaction and ultimate fulfillment in life are both rooted on the way you feel on the inside in relative to the circumstances happening around. Grow beyond the platitude of feelings and develop the attitude of an uncommon genius with a special assignment for her generation. Your worth is in the future, and never in your past. It is a great privilege to be alive to read this. God do not consult your yesterday to bless you at the present and position you at advantage by tomorrow. Unhook your past and prepare for a great future now.

- All it takes to stay relevant to the future is "Phronesis" (wisdom) and "epignosis" (invoke yourself with responsiveness) to dominate your world and be in fortune and in fame. Feeling is like a cap – you drop off one and pick up a matching one that is most relevant to the prevailing circumstances of your life, and are in total control of the outcome of any situation. What you feel about your bad yesteryears is a fact of life but have no power to determine your results or performance

– today, except if you decide to be captive of your ghost past.

- Woman, to be on top is a great task that requires absolute focus on your future, not on yesterday. It is important you guide your words as they jumps out of your lips. Make no mistake, not to wrap it up with golden intentions, because words are sources of life, and it never die no matter the years. Guide your heart with all diligence as wrong words from others can create everlasting damage in your life. It is wisdom if you never say anything you do not want to hear about for the rest of your life. That is the secret you need to sustain your career at the top tomorrow.

- Leadership is so many great ways about results you generated while combining people, resources and time over a given period. If you are not getting desired results, it is possible you have exposed yourself to the wrong influences, then this must discontinue if you must generate a positive outcomes from your effort. Choosing the right
-
- people to expose yourself to is a principal decision of true leadership depending on your ability to clearly define the path you want to follow in life. Never forget in a hurry, pathways determine actual results you achieve at the end of the day.

- People are living pathways that you can leverage on to get to your paradise. It is important you discover who is the golden connection that could shorten your struggles in life; and land you into "recrementitious" (surplus), and make you be in your dream world. Be "makarios" (blessed) beyond your wildest imagination. Recognize the path and recognize the person.

THE ULTIMATE FREEDOM OF WOMANHOOD IN THE KNOWLEDGE AGE

There is a sense and gauge of security in the nudity of a woman in the short run, but the ultimate victory lies in what she does in the equation of resources and prevailing circumstances around her. There is no anagogic abracadabra to gain tight and sustainable security if she cannot turn into cash the latent potentials within her. Whatever life demands from you is already provided for – it is your duty to search it out and roll in great success.

The Knowledge Age thrives in knowledge and never in the "pants -down" of any woman. It is wrong to engage in marathon sex hawking just o make ends-meet when you have great knowledge out there on the streets looking for a mental intercourse to birth you a desire dream and flush you with money, fame and fortune

The ultimate freedom of a woman is not outside her marriage but sure within her. Not in the statistics of what is happening around the corner, rather in the stars of choices that she is making around the corners of the globe. To be in security is a choice you make and never a chance that shows up from the void. The wisdom Age, presents a level playing field for all and sundry who believe on their endowments to encounter destiny.

In the wisdom Age, Success is not a function of your location in the world, instead an import of your consistent devotion to a definite course with clear vision. It is not who engage you that matters but what purpose is driving you around? Women who dare live for purpose lives longer and have more productive results than their contemporaries.

It is important you have people talk and often discus about you – it is a sign that you are investing your time on purpose. The ultimate freedom is not in the abundance at your disposal, but in the ability to live for your purpose of existence. It is your purpose that connects you to be helpers, favour and desired platforms to parade your wares in the marketplaces of life.

A purpose-drive woman is one living in her maximum security, controlling her "acts" and "arts" while living to the fullness of her potentials. You can be the bread winner of the home but never come in content with your true purpose in life. It is your principal assignment to go after your purpose in life. The bread kills with time but purpose discovered, developed, and deployed to work creates unlimited dividends in lifetime.

The day you find purpose, you surely move away from the brothel. It is purpose that keeps people after being through a season of ill-luck, ill-fated marriage, deceit, stacks of losses, and death of beloved one. It is purpose that connects you to your ultimate freedom in life. It is purpose that keeps you walking towards your dream, even when there is no sign of victory in-view. A woman is a creature of purpose! Discover it and live.

It is wrong to build your whole life around a mortal man when you have the privilege to hang on a Divine purpose. Financial freedom is not same thing as everlasting freedom. Financial education or intelligence creates financial freedom; and total submission to the Lordship of Jesus Christ guarantees an eternal freedom. The later is the ultimate freedom, and if you miss out on it, fore SURE – you did miss out on great destiny cum purpose.

The fear of God is the beginning of wisdom and the prelude to connecting to true purpose of your existence. Salvation from sin, and mortal wickedness of men: worth more than the purest of gold in the Buckingham Palace. Salvation from the low life and from eternal damnation is the ultimate dominion of humanity with sagacity of uncommon purpose. It is important you wake up to this profound reality in when you still have mind in place.

Our world is in dire need for leaders with parade of solutions to restore the dignity of man on planet earth. The problem of middle-east is never a political or religious orchestration but as a result of disunity of human purposes. For when the purpose of anything is not known abuse is inevitable.

LAW OF PERCEPTION

Womanhood comes in volumes of perception/perspectives, yet with good character and healthy ideological stand, any woman can serve her world with true conduct and candor. The real difference between a "House Wife" and a "Home Maker" is not in the physical anatomy but in ideology and understanding of each woman. That is exactly where the ultimate freedom lies between every woman irrespective of her location, background or literacy.

A good character is a signature that is not hidden anywhere in the world. You may have a phenomenal success, but you need character to sustain it. Good character is an intangible asset of any woman that fill her world with all her desires, character quotient refers to the degree of moral qualities that has the logical capacity to position you at advantage to get ahead of others in the world – market places. No success is in-view on the absence of a good character.

Every fame, fortune and victory anywhere has "character-bond", and any woman that is on top of career-has network of good and accessible characters. True wealthy of womanhood is both tangible and intangible in value, it is delight to the minds of many and light to the pathways of true greatness in life; womanhood is the "audacity of hope" of mankind .... ask Barrack OBAMA.

Build up your potentiality in this belief and live by apocalypse (revelation) of this **“Risorgimento”** (revival) to create a vent of cornucopia of the universe and fulfill your purpose for living.

Not so many women really understand the significance of image before the public glare. It is truth that clothes is made for the coverage of the skin; still it speaks volumes in the ears of the public. I strongly believe that whatever a woman is willing enough to show to the public, she will likely share with them. The modern day fashion has somehow taken something very significant away from womanhood. Most clothing demean the purpose of humanity, especially that of womanhood. The plus size women pant is good regalia that show off your kind and your etiquette.

Plus size is a signature of a kind, a statement of inestimable value and immensity of treasure on any woman. It makes you feel comfortable and inspire confidence deep down in your mind. A figure-8-shaped woman usually sport well rounded bust line, firm, voluptuous and sultry pounds of flesh that can sedate even a priest on solemn duty.

Wearing
a plus size on this kind of body configuration bears a semblance on special assignment of some sort. It makes you the panorama of many eyes. Before men, eyes are popping out of the skull, projecting and mentally probing into the tiny fantasy of some pleasurable unprintable. It is really the pleasure of most figure-8-shaped ladies to dress on a plus size pant to uncommon parties. It is quiet enchanting!

It is important one dresses according to her shape and not according to sheer inclination of fashion. What is in vogue is not important when it comes to actual dressing to look fine and pretty. You have to opt for a custom-made plus size pant or top that can trace your figure and make you proud of yourself. Such make you walk with flamboyance, panache and poise to rule your day and your world with air of great importance. You see yourself dilly-dally into the orbits and flash with hilarious smiles to woo whoever you want on your fleet.

To a plus size figure-8-shaped lady she rules her world with elegance and beauty. She is the pride of her mate and the bright morning star of his shine before his friends. The husband of a plus size figure-8-shaped lady always exudes with charisma that can intimidate an angel on duty in the Buckingham palace, because his woman has actually discovered herself in the world of exceptional fashion of the century.

POETIC...

SAGACITY OF

WOMANHOOD

THE PLATINUM LOVE

Never say die in the morning while Mr. Platinum moans with glow,
Never say stop in the noon while Mr. Platinum is nude in the shimmer of his own sweat,
Never say sing in the evening while Mr. Platinum doodles in lulu rhythm,
Never say sleep in the night, while Mr. Platinum smacks aglow,
Never say wake at mid-night because Mr. Platinum is dreaming green love.

I hold you in my illusion; kiss you in my allusion,
Never say go my love, I am green with love,
I hold you in my arms; wrap you with the labyrinth of my heart,
Never say greening with the lips, love speaks in my house,
Love is dreaming in my arms, sitting in pleasure within my hearts,
Smack me high aglow in the reminiscence of my dream,
Love is aglow with pleasure without measure,

My love is pale tonight but full in ecstasy of the morning,
Moaning is pleasure, higher than the highest of the fissure,
Though in my serenity I feel rarity in this reality,
Platinum love glows with green shine, brighter than the brightest of the morning.

I hear a deep sound of music in her house; music is sweeter in the morning,
Moaning is sweeter in the morning, Holy Grail…pots of pits,
Not for the unmarried lest the fall of the holy Priest,
Not for children less the holy grail of truth smack the earth with a bang,
Not for the infidel less Satan orbit the planet Heaven,
Not for apes less the corruption of human serum,
Not for the bride of error….the ancient of holocaust
Not for the price, it is a prize of faithfulness,
Not for the groom of impatient, it is the beauty of honey moon,
Not for pang, my platinum love is real a meal of gem,
Plant me a kiss, gat me on planet 'P' suit Platinum.
Love is the blood in flowing in my vein, flowing from my eyes.
I dream the dream of green, platinum love is aglow with green

NATURE

Dream my love only if you have the heart,
Dream my love even in disgust and emptiness,
Dream my love even in a lost land,
Dream my love even in a hole,
Dream my love even on top of Mount Everest,
Dream my love even on empty stomach,

My Love is green, a symbol of fertility, and a tiara of hope,
No one can give away than my love; none has the passion of love,
My Love has the power to make, save and give hope to the dying people,
My Love makes the World to go round.

My love is green, greener than the Federal Reserve,
My love know no bounds,
My love hates derivatives of derivatives,
My love is worth far more than greenish Dollar,
My love is on a mission impossible,
My heart is broken for love; I cannot feel my impulse,
My heart is white; my love is purer than the purest of gold,

Love is Green, the colour of fertility of Mother Nature,
No one hangs on the cross of crucifix, except if him abodes with love,
Love has patience, kindness as surname and sacrifice as second skin to the body,
Love is Green, the golden pearl of greatness,
The missing adventure of infidel, the missing note of terrorist,
Indomitable weaponry to fight hatred, Love is life,

Dream my love even in the whitest of white,
Dream my love even in the greenest of green,
Dream my love even in the darkest of the dark,
Dream my love even in the bluest of the blues,
Dream my love even in the yellowiest of yellow,
Dream my love even in the reddest of the red,
Dream my love even in the colorless of colours

MARRIAGE

My Love is green with passion and fiery with emotion,
My Love is green with flame to burn the orchard of numbness,
My Love is green with aglow to radiate the pathway of lustfulness,
My Love is green with speed to bridge the vast chasm of the earth,
My love is borderless, shimmers with a shine, glows on globe of life,
Hands on lap of keys, eyes on the crystal of light, mind walks daruru,
(Daruru is the author word for helter-skelter)

My feet refuse to carry me on my ride to luliendom of wild enrichindom,
My eyes is caught in the web cluster of coral of Cordoba,
My eyes on marriage of thoughts smoldering under intense cuddle,
Marry Mary make merry of marriage of masks in Mulley Magna,

My dream one comes from Magnesia to make magnetic signature,
Marriage is the hub, nay, orb of life, Simmers with flame of consummation of sultry passion. Dream my Green love on your marriage night.

"Tiddy-taddy" shuffles the heart filled with alluring passion,
The feet dilly-dally flat on the slab of allusion, euphoria over my heart,
I am lost in Bermuda triangle because of love nitty-gritty,
My sweet heart comes from afar to make love with my marriage diary,
My marriage is my dream come true even in prime of crisis,
My sweet one makes love like never before but without a garrison carrot,
My dream is my dream; my green is my growing deep and deeper in allure,
My love is green with Pleroma of Chara.

Honey my soul to the abyss my darling one,
Honey my soul to Las Vegas there my love goes aglow,
Honey me to my weakest crest –the plateau of platitudes,
Honey my soul holy Maya- orb of elemental adroitness,
Honey my soul oh rainbow of love, green is my color code,

Green in my soul, love on my skin,
Green in my dream, my love is green,
Green in my soul, dreams my green love.

Romance Curriculum for Knowledge age

"THE FIVE TESTS OF LOVE"

Love is blind they say, but I believe marriage is an eye opener. The institution of marriage in the today world is at the verge of hitting a shipwreck and go into shambles as there are many wrong people in marriages. It is imperative to develop this golden mindset at the onset of any relation; that, marriage is not meant for boys but for men, and not meant for girls, but for women. I will be handling mine wrong personalities in both relationship and marriage that you should avoid in my next write up. But my fundamental mission here is to help you asses your man or woman on the following parameters below:

1. ADMIRATION TEST: - Your man or woman must love you enough to de-emphasize your "odds" and magnify your "adds", that is your "pluses" If there is anything like that in the dictionary. His or her love must be strong enough to write off your physical and charismatic deficiencies and cherish for the way God has made you unique in your own world. But, if he or she often gets critical about your size, face, looks and carriage, then, his/her admiration quotient for is low. Should you plunge ahead to contract your marriage with such a person, then, one day you hit the waterloo of divorce. Take time to find out how often he or she uses the following phrases:

- I love your face…

- I am proud of you...
- I am thrill whenever you show up...
- You are my angel...
- I am taking you out for a party...
- I am taking you for games...
- Wear that your pink clothes or T-Shirt
- Etc

It is truth that words are deceitful, especially in the sugar-coated tongues of selfish lover only seeking for what is beneath the panties.

Albeit; a true lover, who is proud of you will always admire you before friends, family members, and in the public. A selfish lover will only tell you these words on phone, email and behind close doors

2. GIVING TEST: Love is more of giving and less of taking from the traditional perspective, the man is expected to be in the business of giving while the woman is often saddled with the responsibility of receiving. Little wonder why, the woman is often trapped with pregnancy during courtship in the relationship. The pre-occupation of receiving and taking virtually everything ranging from tangible to intangible put the woman into a vulnerable position to find it difficult to resist pre-marital sex whenever the man want to give her this level of affection.

In the contemporary view of relationship, the two people involved must make commitment to giving to each other irrespective of financial or social status. The two must help each other whenever necessity demands for that. If the guy shops for this week, you can shop reciprocate by shopping for him next week, even if it is just buying him a T-shirt or handkerchief. One thing is sure about gift; it speaks volumes and reflects both personality and mindset. In true relationship there is no parameter

to ascertain gift or giving when both parties are actively involved. Giving actually is a mindset, and does not depict wealth or riches.

COMMUNICATION TEST: Communication is everything in both relationship and marriage for a woman. From research women speaks an average of

70,000 words every 24 hours while men speaks barely 12,000 words daily. Woman by design have their greatest power in the mouth, and therefore, have flare to talk about everything whether sensible or not, and that is the sole reason they can stay with five to twelve children in the house from morning till evening. This is an uncommon grace- that men do not have. To keep your marriage or relationship you have to keep talking with your woman. What destroys relationship and marriages is talking at your lover. For Christ sake, talk with him or her often.

Using silence as a weapon against your lover in a relationship or marriage is the easiest way to welcome the monster of break-up or divorce to invade the honey therein. A man's silence means several things to a woman, and being emotionally crafted the woman can pull the trigger that will destroy that relationship or marriage. Just keep talking with your partner on any topic whether it makes sense or not. "1+1=1" is even nonsense, but in marriage or relationship it is high sense. Friend, watch who is talking often with your woman before her heart is stolen from you. Women are emotional just as children, the guy who is fast and smart at talking and telling those funny folk tales will surely steal the heart of your woman. For a woman communication is everything, and for a man who must keep his relationship or marriage-endeavor to hype your communication quotient. There is nothing like I am not giving to talking that much. OYO! "On your-own" my brother, it is far better you talk more with her than filling her account with rubies.

3. TRUST TEST: Enter into a relationship that is geared towards marriage or rather contract marriage with some that you can trust. Abuse of trust or lack of it has thwarted several love relationships and marriages prematurely. Visit the welfare, abuse of trust or absence of it breaks down roughly estimate of 75% of all divorced or dissolved marriages. You cannot build a good relationship or marriage on suspicion. Do away with any partner you cannot trust as broken relationship is both cheaper and better than broken marriage. The only way you can have a trustworthy relationship or marriage is to become trustworthy yourself. Score yourself today to know your trust quotient.

Check out the following.

- Can you be trusted with another woman/man in same house that is not a blood relative to you, but a friend of your woman or man?
- Can you keep your sanity on the absence of your partner?
- Can you keep your sanity despite the fact, women or men flock around you often (as you claims)?
- Can you keep yourself undefiled till the night after your wedding?

Note, more than 65% of marriages contracted on the altar of pre-marital sex often hit the corridors of welfare for divorce or dwells in suspicious as each partners suspects the other on infidelity. Pre-marital sex breeds infidelity and lack of trust in marriage. I advise you walk down the isle with someone you trust so much without atom of suspicion and make sure your both trust quotient is compatible to keep you in the marital ship for life.

4. EMOTIONAL TEST: It is said that man comes from Mars and that woman comes from Venus, but the good thing is that both live on planet earth. Men and women can contend in the world of professionalism and Charismatic prowess, but come to the climate of love- it is a different ball game altogether. The women come into a relationship or marriage with myriads of emotions to love and to be loved, but men approach love with a rational mind.

Naturally, women do not shop ulterior motives when it come to demonstrating love to their partner, but men usually shop for several things in the convolution of their minds while demonstrating love. Only time will unravel a man actual intentions behind his actions and inactions while in a relationship with a woman. It is unfortunate that men who are cowards often take advantage of a woman one dimensional approach to relationship or marriage. As emotionally designed being the woman is often fast to give up her nudity and body to man that she loves, but the man, nay, coward lick his fingers, explore and exploit the woman, then, borrow "Ben Johnson". If he stays, then, it is to make caricature of the partner, and remind her that there are more plenty ladies out their waiting for him. This is wrong!

Before you think of going into any relationship or contracting marriage with anyone, take time to decipher how your partner worth or cherish your emotions. Check whether he or she is emotional compatible without sporting ulterior motives. If your partner asks for sex before marriage, ask why. If your partner tells you that having sex or outright indulgence in pre-marital sex will build up formidable bond between you both- show him the way to brothels. Often a time, when the coward boy makes a porn star out of you, he reduces both your value and your chances to live happy ever after. Trust your emotions into the right hand cage the animalistic impulses within you and wait for the right time to explore your emotions. It is the golden way to stay married and happy after.

NINE POTENTIAL DANGERS YOU NEED TO AVOID IN RELATIONSHIP OR IN MARRIAGE

The key to long lasting and happy marriages is not so much in finding the right person but in being the right person. Marriage is not all about sex marathon or material embellishment rather is in the first place a sacred institution ordained by God though managed by man. It is important you don't "fall in love". You need not to shut your eyes to obvious realities that threaten relationships across the globe, and that can easily tear your hearts apart in the future. It is against this background that I want to discuss in details the nine potential dangers you need to avoid in relationships or marriage:

1. Do not tie the nuptial at the altar if there exist persistent lack of trust between two of you: No matter the financial gain you stand to get if you walk down the aisle to tie the nuptial at the altar if there is a lingering lack of trust for your partner, it is better and cheaper you quit the relationship. A broken engagement is better than a broken marriage. Money cannot build trust into a relationship because trust is an intangible asset of a person that boosts his character quotient in both business and relationship respectively.

2. If you spend most of the time with your partner disagreeing and quarrelling: This is a typical sign of a relationship that must crumble just with time. It is

better you spend time studying and building up one another in conversation and in prayer. Watch out for couples that quarrels and disagrees often, they do not make happy homes and blissful union at the end of the day. It is important that you agree at the onset to help each other build up missing values and character. You do not quarrel to win a medal so it is not even necessary, rather identify your weak points and be plain to accept constructive criticism from your partner. If you happen to have the inefficiencies that can trigger a divorce in marriage it is important you seek for both expert and godly counsels from right persons respectively.

3. If your Partner insists that you drop all your old friends and start a fresh in building a social life that matches "his" or "hers: This is a major signal that there is a boiling point waiting for explosion in the near future. It

is better you find a way to resolve this issue amicably with you partner or dissolve the relationship to save yourselves of emotional trauma in the near future.

4. If either of you continue to ruminate within the question like- is he or she really sure about the love for me "he" or "she" professes: This is nothing but significant element of doubt that shops the capacity to build up to explosive potential in the near future. The spirit of doubt suspects everything in relationship and suspects even it. It is a typical oddity in relationship that be seriously dealt with before it spreads its poisonous tentacles. If you do not love the person or you perceive that he or she do not love you, there is not need to pretend for whatever reason, simply ask for exist to save you both of heartbreak in the future. However, I must not hesitate to inform you that true love is blind gradually and cannot be perfected

instantaneously. It is better you take time to put in everything that will develop the love, then, if your doubt persist predicate upon your outcomes so far you can parachute away from the love garden.

5. If you are marrying for the wrong reason- like money, affluence, beauty, handsomeness, etc: Marriage is not about glamour but realities of bliss in giving and receiving between two matured persons who are most suitable and compatible to each other. Affluence, beauty, money and handsomeness including host of others can fade away into the void with time. It is only marriage that is contracted on agape love that can stand the test of time. Good name, good character track record of good interpersonal relationship in both associates and business, and God-fearing are all great gains and pluses that any good marriage can be

build upon. Every other thing should be secondary or addition to these solid bricks of marriage foundation.

6. If you both are under-age (I.e. less than 20 years): it is truth that age in the 21st century is no more a function of number but a thing of the mind. Despite this truism, marriage is an eye opener and not a laboratory to test hypotheses of this status. It is far better you both have gone beyond 23yrs or more to build reasonable emotional shock absorbers to tolerate each other idiosyncrasies

7. If you are actually marrying someone to mother or father you; you need a wife not a mother and a husband not a father for a partner: North-South, West-East, people marry within their age range and only few go outside their age bracket to marry. It is a matter of what your ultimate ambition or expectation in marriage is, that really determine who you marry. It

is wise to marry for your conviction devoid of future crisis potential.

8. If both of you are not spiritually compatible: Before you say I do, take your time to find out what your partners belief system or values is like. You must have compatible spiritual background if you contract your marriage. It is extremely difficult to merge a Christian and a Moslem in a marriage union no matter the level of readiness on both sides. It is only time that will unravel disaster looming in the shadowy.
9. if both of you are temperamentally compatible; Most marital union dissolved into waters of divorce on the ground that couples could not complement each

other's temperament. It is usually difficult to have two high tempered people come together for marriage that will see its first decade after wedding

3 WRONG PERSONALITIES TO AVOID IN MARRIAGE

Personality is a character trait that has both natural and nurtured (i.e. acquired) perspective. Naturally people grow up in certain environment to pick up wrong and negative character traits from others in the environment. If such trait is nurtured overtime consciously or unconsciously the individual begin to have problem with others as they find his character and carriage repulsive. Such a person will hardly last long in any relationship. Some people on the other hand are born with wrong character traits that can be cultured but if uncultured will become a problem to the bearer and those he encounters in relationship in his journey of life.

Below are (2) two wrong personalities to avoid in marriage:-

1. THE ABSENTEE LOVER: - Love between two matured people is to be shared and consummated on the bed of bliss and romance. It is made to support and care for one another, especially in the time of need. The absentee-Lover believes in love from afar or over the internet. He can manage left over and any other woman on your absence. She can also many another man on your absence. One funny thing about absentee-Lover is that he or she is always busy sorting out things.

North-South an absentee-Lover is never to be trusted with a golden future because he or she is not predictable. He can wire you several telephone calls or sends you catalogue of emails, but always giving you horde of excuses why he won't be around for your birthday or date-meeting. An absentee-Lover is a wrong personality in the arena of relationship or marriage. He breaks your heart at the slightest confrontation because he hardily knows your true worth.

The right yardstick to measure love is the time scale. Anyone who cannot devote time to cultivate you love might not have time for you later after marriage. To love is to give but not giving in absence of your presence. Do not make a mistake to open your heart for whatever reason for someone with a shimmering smile, soft spoken voice and looks of

"time-cop" because he will be on the move always to the East or to the West. And that is what I call "Pendulum Lover" because as he
shuttles the ends of the earth so his love dial "to" and "fro" from Nneka in Nigeria to Julia in West Indies, then back to origin which you, probably, at Las Vegas. Absentee-Lover is usually a polygamous lover at the end of the day when all the chips are down. Beware!

2. THE LAZY-BOSS MAN: This is the worst kind of wrong personality in the arena of marriage that you must avoid with all diligence. At first, he or she appears to be so committed to give you all you can ask for, but before you could say: "William Shakespeare" he or she is relaxing to expect you assume the permanent lead. He will expect you to shop for him, assist him pay off his monthly bills, and do domestic for him. She will expect you to take her out all the time without reciprocating your support and care.

Love is all about responsibilities shared by two people involved. Marriage is eternal commitment to shoulder responsibility, but if

one person is a lazy-boss man, then the whole thing becomes a gulf war. A lazy boss man is at home all the time watching movies, playing computer games or watching a dancing bear at the circus. A lazy boss man will not look for work if out of job. He or she will always tell you there is no job for him or her out there. At worst a lazy -boss man can resort to stealing and street hawking of hard drugs. Run away from a lazy - boss man

3. MARRIAGE TO A BIMBO

There is a mistake you will make in life, especially in the arena of marriage that will cause you a lifetime of regrets and sorrow. Marriage to a Bimbo is the single worst mistake many women make in marriage in the 21st century. It has cost many their fortune and hard earned respect in life. It has torn several happy families apart and forces the bread of sorrow down their throats. It is a destiny-destroying mistake that can reduce a lofty personality to a pimp-juice.

A Bimbo is an attractive but unintelligent person moved and concerned only by external beauty and cosmetics. He does not have affinity for self-

improvement of any sort, but believes that sex alone can solve the problems in relationship or marriage. Probably, was not born this way but acquired "**Bimbolism**" by way of nurturing over time. A closer look into his diary will reveal that he has been through serial abused relationships that finally hit a shipwreck, and he is kicked out. He can afford to stay in any relationship despite the abuses and humiliation so long his material needs are met. He has no problem.
He approaches marriage from the materialistic perspective but has little or nothing else to contribute for the sustenance of the marriage.

A Bimbo believes that his sexual prowess is the key to access the riches of his lover or spouse, but can never contribute productively to the welfare of the home. He rather spends much shopping for brandy clothes, necklaces, and shoes than spend on his self improvement. He browses the internet 24hrs and 7days a week to learn the latest fore-play and sex positions, but hardily check out the financial times and economic journals online.

A BIMBO WILL CAUSE YOU THE FOLLOWING SORROWS:

1. Financial Pain: - if you are the lousy type a Bimbo will drain your bank account to shop often for him and sponsor a younger girlfriend to satisfy his sexual cravings on your absence.
2. EMOTIONAL PAIN: - A Bimbo will deny you access to sex if you are not able to meet up with his material needs. The truth is that he will not hesitate to zip down before any fellow who

can afford to take care of his needs, even if it is temporary.

3. HEALTH PAIN: - With his level of frivolity, he can contact diseases and infections which he definitely pass on to you. If you lucky, you will escape the venom of HIV/Aids.

4. FAMILY PAIN: - A Bimbo can throw an entire family into chaos with his selfish activities just to satisfy lust and pleasure. If you are low-income earner and have to work for long hour's daily- a Bimbo Spouse will definitely hang out with any of your willing family member that can afford his slightest need. It is just a matter of time, you will find out that either your elder sister or far younger sibling is sleeping with your proud and handsome Bimbo.

5. ETERNAL PAIN: - If you engage all known wits and wisdom around to keep a Bimbo in marriage, you may later find out that other women outside or friend of yours are having babies for him outside your marriage. At this, you might over-react and shot someone: Sex-maniac or his accomplice, then you book a life jail in the prison yard. Beware! A Bimbo is watching your back.

2 CRITICAL REASONS WHY YOU MUST NOT OPT FOR DIVORCE

The 21st Century streams with surprises almost in every field of life. The most astounding is that of marriage institutions that are fast collapsing into cold waters of divorce. The incessant quest for divorce among married couple across the universal axes is becoming an emerging trend in the sacred institution of marriage. Like new brand of fashion in the shopping mall- every Dick and Harry wants to go to the welfare to dissolve his or her marriage for one unlikely reason or the other. Before you ask for a divorce, take your time to consider the two reasons below as follows:-

1. The kids: - Children are gifts from Heaven and not just product of your body or attestation of your biological healthiness. So many people ask for a divorce or dissolve their marriage on personal reasons for selfish ambition or purpose but without giving a thought to the Psychology and the entire emotional embodiment of the kids. Even some simply walk out of their union without looking at the direction of the kids. At the end of the day, the kids suffer the negative impact of the adult decision. This is a big issue in the 21st century as there is much emphasis to attaining a perfect society. It is a fundamental human right violation of the highest order that many adults are committing this day against the children. What the National Constitution provides in the

welfare of the children for a divorced marriage can naturally never substitute the presence of a real home for these kids. Little wonder if the parents themselves could have grown into something profitable to themselves and to the society without the presence of their real parents living together.

It is important that the welfare seek the consent of the kids before dissolving any marriage even if the adults involved are willing to go separate ways. Just asking the woman to take the custody of the kids and the man to visit them in a while on Court permission is a great crime the society commits against the child standing on the border-line. At that point the child destiny is in jeopardy even in the presence of all welfare provisions and protection. The child need more than food, security and money.

The child needs the support and unrestrained care of both parents. The child is exposed to emotional trauma of some sort without the presence of one parent. This mortal bonding with father and mother is a thing that no amount of care and support of one parent can replace that of the other. The child surely grows up with a missing fundamental element that only a united home can give.

2. THE FUTURE: - It is important couples take time to snap into the future ahead of time to catch a glimpse of what it would look like without the kids. The future is pregnant with surprises because anything can happen to deny one joy for a life time. To obtain divorce is as easy as signing the register for attendance in a workshop, but not so easy when time begins to invent certain packages of surprises to you in the near future. The kids can grow up into adulthood to hate you or even denounce you as a biological parent.

The child can grow up into a bloody sadist and one day cut across your way to murder you because of the hatred life has shown him for your selfish decision to walk away when or she needed you most. On the other hand, the kid can grow up into a big superstar in any field of life but will not cherish to have you in his or her company for whatever reason you had to walk out on him or her at the prime of life. These are important reasons that couples should consider before breaking up.

HOW TO INTERPRETE THE MALE IN YOUR PARTNER AND BREAK DOWN THE BARRIERS IN YOUR SEX LIFE

- DRIVE: - Every man drive is outward. He has invested his energy, time and pride in places other than the home- in his job and business. It is wise if you do not Mis-interpret his drive as complete neglect of your person or effort attending to issues in the home. It is just a display of sheer maleness. If your partner does not show enthusiasm for putting up a clean curtain or repairing a drippy faucet, just know that this is the male in him. With this understanding in place you break down every barrier of emotional devastation to enjoy the bliss of your marriage.

- **THE HOUSE IS YOUR BUSINESS:** - For the man his career, office or business is the extension of his personality. The house is extension of the woman personality. You do not have to be tempted to miss-judge your partner if he takes it for granted that you keep his home neat and clean. He may not notice the clean cushions, curtains and neat rug or floor. Most men do not even perceive the sweet-smelling air freshener in the sitting room, hardly appreciate the well arranged chairs and electronics and ironed clothing on the kids. Make no mistake, this is not an indication of his lack of love for you and the family it is just about the male thing in him. It is universal, only few men take time to re-condition themselves in order to woo their spouses, and win their love over and over again. The fact remains that every real man appreciates having his home and kids in the competent hands of an understanding woman. It is not weakness of some sort… it is just "male"

- WHAT TURNS HIM ON? Sex is another area in which most married women or those in intimate relationship misunderstand men. Men are easily turned on by sights, sounds, odours and slight touch of a woman. You may feel that this characteristic trait programs him to be amorous and lack control over his zip. It is manly to appreciate a beautiful woman, respond to allure of a woman giggle and get charmed by scent a woman is wearing, and still keep your gun under your pants. Most women find this difficult to believe about their men. They believe that once a man start passing pleasantries to another woman or appreciate her beauty or enchanting perfume- he is weak and should not be trusted. This is wrong judgment.

Give your man that benefit of doubt of his manliness in this area, and still keep watching if he is giving this fellow unnecessary and undue attention. Then, you need to pull the buttons for caution, because too much familiarity brings content. It is even better to study the things that turn him on often in women and fortify yourself in this regard to keep for yourself alone. Naturally, men who have themselves under control will not allow the revealing nakedness of a woman outside, sights, sounds and perfume to stimulate them.

This is more possible with a godly and spirit filled men. I therefore, call on you take your man to church if you really love him much and want him by your side for life. You can as well encourage your man to read more of fictionally epics to occupy his mind with something else.

WHY MEN MAKE LOVE TO FACES...... THE REAL STORY BEHIND THE SCENE

The worst mistake so many women are making in this 21st century is neglect of their faces. The facial impression matters too much to a man and is usually the point of call of every man. The face is suppose to be the strongest weapon of any woman has against a man. To have beautiful and right facial endowments makes you the queen of your man kingdom only if you know how to create right signatures with it at right time or in seasons. If you cannot tap the magic of your face in your relationship, then, it is better you do not have one in the first place.

The worst or ugliest kind of face rightly manipulated can strip the holy apron away from the priest and rock him very to stand confused like Egyptian mummy before the sacrament. This is not a sign of weakness or unmanliness as some women may tend to misjudge. It is just the male thing in every man. Godly fearing men has His (i.e. God) spirit in dwelling in them to cage this adamic nature even before Vegas Strippers. But is better, the man in the first place is not exposed to this oddity. There is always a 100% tendency to react in line with the sight of a rustic face shimmering with spell of connubiality.

Naturally, men make love to faces when it comes to sex and reaching orgasmic platitude. Every man bears the beast of lust within that must be cultured less it send the man down to his early grave. It is this best that snaps the pictures of faces and builds upon it by involuntary reactions of the mind convolutions to set up a call of nature which is the sole responsibility of every man to constantly put in check or tamed.

I have beard and handled cases of sexual misadventure of some married folks who can only gain erection strong enough to pleasure their woman by looking out a picture of a woman on the walls of their bedroom. Some people will like to watch or behold naked pictures of beautiful porn stars to reach orgasm while making love to their legitimate wife. This is arrant nonsense and unethical in any marriage. It has broken down several homes as the woman sees herself reduced to object to fulfill a sexual therapy or craze of the man. Every woman wants to be really loved and appreciated always.

A lady in her 40s injured her husband with iron rod for mistakenly calling or mincing an unknown name while making love to her. When she noticed this, she pushed him off and hit him with her shoes. The man sustained terrible injury from this misadventure. After close investigation into the issue the lady found out that, that name was actually that of a mistress in the neighborhood. The marriage suffered terrible crises, and hit the rock of divorce two months later.

Several marriages have ended just this way either as a result of the man or the woman fault.

Most men actually contracted marriage just because the woman is beautiful to behold without even giving a second thought on the character behind such face. Women also make same mistake when they are caught by the charm of Macho biceps of the man which may just be opposite in character behind the man meaning. It is important you watch closely on you man to know who is stealing his attention from you. But do not be suspicions

The diary of the wealthiest Woman a life

- **There is enough for everyone**:_- There is more than enough in the universe beyond what anyone can assume. The problem of the universe is not non-existent of abundant supply of all things, but not enough demand of all that are available in the cosmos cornucopian of wealth. To access the treasury of the universe, you must become an ardent seeker of the principle that governs supply of whatever you desire and able to demand for it effectively and passionately.
- Money is a symbol of substance: - Life endowed humanity with surplus-substances. There is never a shortage of substance anywhere in the world or in the history of mankind on the planet earth. There is no tree that grows money, but you can harness the money

potentials locked up in any tree. There is superabundance of money locked in the nature in our environment, events and seasons of life. This is only made possible by the brain power of man to recognize this goldmine around us. You can live in unlimited supply of desired riches if you can engage your mind resourcefully at work in the cosmic storehouse.

- Search for wealth from inside first: - It is a mistake of the 19th and 20th century to program the minds of men to search for riches outside, instead of starting first from the deep within the man. Wealth is a resultant of rich mind and not a magic of poor mind vacillating with tiny paper certificate. The industrial age programmed men to worship paper qualifications even if the man carrying such certificates is not satisfied by the accomplishment of this tool kit. It is far better to search for wealth from inside first before considering any tangible option. The worst economic condition does not regard academic qualifications, but prostrate in obedience before rich mind with a rich plan of action.

- Creative ideas create wealth: - You can become rich if you become creative at heart. You become very rich if you dare put into action your ideas; and you can become extraordinary rich if you can keep recycling same idea over and over again. You can stay very rich all through your life-time if you stay consistent on your action to put your ideas to work.
- The richest is a diligent hand: - Excuses are excuses, but performance is golden. The world will celebrate you if you commit yourself to make it a better place for all. The richest people on earth do not own the biggest factory or produce the biggest products in the market place, but have enough creative idea that they pursue with all

diligence till it begin to churn out solution that the world will pay for to have.

- ❖ Ignorance is malignant of the mind; and as a free moral agent, you have the power to accept or resist it. It is your sole responsibility to seek and secure the knowledge and wisdom that empower you to live a happy, prosperous, distinguished and accomplished life on planet earth. Just echo within you this mantra: "I can make it happen".

EPILOGUE:

If a woman is hot, it is good if the hotness harness the potentials lucked up in her brain than reduce her true value at the market place. Hot quickie produces hot outcomes, and heated romantic pleasure produces hated regretful treasure a times. Womanhood is the hub of humanity that orbits the future constellations of any generation and for all sapience sense. Have the sixth sense but not the sixth insatiable sense of sensuality. Have a strong affinity to show love to others, but not lovemaking in TV commercials.

- Womanhood is the ageless epitome of love, and remains the pristine crown of humanity on planet earth wrapped in

- succulent vessel, loaded with psychological hype, clothed with voluptuous flesh, red with love, pale with mind emotions, pregnant with burdens of cares, and speaks with distinctive excellence that fills the ambience with ebullience of sapience – is the creature called WOMAN!.

ABOUT AUTHOR:

Ritchie Felix is a Prolific Writer, a Medallion Award winner, a Poet, a Novelist, an Essayist, impeccable Story Teller of note, Corporate Re-branding Expert, Business Consultant, a trained Physicist, ICt4D and e-payment solution Expert, a highly sought after Conference Speaker of Note, e-commerce Consultant, Poverty Reduction cum Eradication Specialist. He has created several Businesses and Products, and helped many organizations dominate their Market Niche.

Ritchie Felix's Specialties:

- Business & Personal Development
- Youth Development Strategist
- Wealth Creation using ICT4D simple tools
- Security intelligence & Stardom Management
- Online Publications
- Life Coaching
- Human Rights Advocacy

OTHER BOOKS BY RITCHIE FELIX

- THE JUNGLE SAGE
- INCOME EDGE
- THE APOCALYPSE
- THE CREATURE FROM EGYPTIAN PYRAMID
- THE STREET MILLIONAIRE
- YOUNG, SMART & SEXY
- SAGACITY OF THE SMARTEST & HIGHLY EFFECTIVE PEOPLE
- WEALTH ORACLE
- ROMANCE CURRICULUM
- MOTIVATIONAL EDGE FOR YOUNG PEOPLE
- AUDACITY OF CHANGE
- THE CRYSTAL BALL

www.ingramcontent.com/pod-product-compliance
Lightning Source LLC
Chambersburg PA
CBHW072047280526
45788CB00006B/2209

* 9 7 8 1 4 5 2 8 1 9 8 1 5 *